Experience Poems and Pictures

Anna J. Small Roseboro

Interspersed with my poems are pictures of
artwork arranged alphabetically
by last name of artist.

EXPERIENCE POEMS AND PICTURES
Published by Anna J. Small Roseboro
© 2019 by Anna J. Small Roseboro

Art on Cover Design
Highland Lake
by Susan J. Osborn
Oil on Paper
22" x 28"

All rights reserved. Printed in the United States of America. No part of this book may be reproduced, or stored in a retrieval system, or transmitted in any form or by any means, electronic, mechanical, or photocopying, recording or otherwise, without express written permission of the author.

www.teachingenglishlanguagearts.com

Plutarch quotation from *Brainy Quotes*
https://www.brainyquote.com/quotes/plutarch_117780

Artists whose work appears in this publication have consented to have pictures of their artwork printed with my poems.
Artists retain rights to their original work.

Some of my poems have appeared
in earlier print and electronic publications.

The "Entering Art" activities are based on my notes from a workshop led by Terry and Jenny Williams
at the Detroit Institute of Art.

Copyright 2019
Anna J. Small Roseboro
ISBN: 9781096784753

Dedication

to God, my inspiration; my husband, William Gerald Roseboro;
my children: Roz, Bill and Bob; my siblings; my extended
family, and my friends who encourage and support me.

to writers who, like me, find that writing is a way
to explore, expand, and explain experiences,
to capture in words and keep near to our hearts
those in our lives who are dear to us.

Acknowledgements

Heartfelt thanks for the blessings of assistance from
Claudia Marschall, co-editor-sister
Susan Osborn, friend, colleague, and collaborator
Elizabeth Wepsic and her students from The Bishop's School
Brooke Suiter, friend, reader, and colleague
Laury Isenberg, friend, colleague, and patroness
Verneal Y. Mitchell, sister and beta reader.

All the artists whose work you will experience here.

TABLE OF CONTENTS

POEM	ARTIST	TITLE
10		Words, Words, Words
PICTURE		
12	Jayamini Attanayake	*The Family*
		Grampoppa
POEMS A		
14		Acquainted with That Song
16		Ballad of William and Ann
20		Waiting, Waiting, Waiting
22		Phillis Wheatley Told Me
PICTURES A		
24	Deanna Denby Beye	*Garden Door*
		Garden Wall
26	Mary Clendeninn	*Cathedral Windows*
		January Gemstone: Garnet
28	Moya Devine	*Summer and Rootbeer*
		The Snake Charmer
30	Nicole Ellsworth	*Native*
		Cascade
32	Annie Fang	*Falling Leaves*
		Regression 2
34	Rachel Galarneau	*View from Clear Lake*
		Purple Haze
POEMS B		
36		Summer Storm
38		Poor, Pluto, Indeed!
40		Sounds on an Evening Walk
42		Romeo Rap: Timeless and Timely
44		The Heart Tree
46		Fist Fighting

PICTURES B	Page		Titles
	48	Nilly Gill	*Fresh off the Press*
			Heat
	50	Therese Cipiti Herron	*Belvedere*
			Summer
	52	Ellie Hodges	*Letting Go*
			Self Portrait
	54	Nathan Huynh	*Rebel Youth*
			Distinguished Gentleman
	56	Steven Kelly	*Time Relative*
			Strands of Life
	58	Layla Khazeni	*Submersion*
			Recovery
	60	Luna Kostic	*Torn*
			Filter
	62	Laura Lehman	*Memories*
			Drama

POEMS C			
	64		Grammama
	66		Our Son
	70		Visits

PICTURES C	Page		Titles
	76	Christie Linnard	*Track and Field*
			Puffer
	78	Linda Moe	*Communication*
			Old Road
	80	Thia Nevius	*The Wish*
			Three Friends
	82	Susan J. Osborn	*Cut Up*
			Picador
	84	Eric Pan	*Broken Pieces*
			Grandfather Lǎo Yé
	86	Carlyssa Phoon	*Croc*
			Bear
	88	Stephen Steele	*Conduit #1*
			Second Hand Rapture

POEMS D
90	The Man with the Holes in His Socks
94	Anniversary Poem
96	The Evening Walk

PICTURES D
100	Sabrina Tian	*Self Portrait – Illiteracy*
		Untitled
102	Minnie Valero	*La Clef (The Key)*
		La Tranquera (The Gate)
104	Elizabeth Wepsic	*Cottage*
		Hidden Passage
106	Lester White	*Shadow of Knowledge I*
		Shadow of Knowledge II
108	Nancy White	*Walking to the Game*
		Ireland
110	Marcus Woolley	*Map #1*
		Map #2
112	Sharisa You	*Depreciated*
		Floral Dance

POEM
114	Yes, You Are!

REFLECTIONS
116	Reflecting on Experiences with Poems and Pictures
118	Entering Art and Writing About It
121	Writing Stories about Pictures
124	Writing a Pantoum Poem about a Picture
125	Exploring Poems to Create Art

WEBSITES
Artists
Poet

"Painting is silent poetry, and poetry is painting that speaks." Plutarch

Words, Words, Words

Words stir me
When I hear them,
When I read them,
When I write them,
When I speak them.

Words urge me
To keep listening
To keep reading
To keep writing
To keep speaking.

Let me hear you,
so I can know you.
Let me speak,
so you can know me.

Prodigiously stirring words
help me know you.
And viscerally urging words
help me know me.

February, 2001

The Family
Jayamini Attanayake
Watercolor
9" x 12"

Grampoppa
Jayamini Attanayake
Watercolor
9" x 12"

Acquainted with That Song

I have been one acquainted
    with that song.
I've sung the song in tune and out of tune.
I have held that high note
    oh so long.

I have sung that song –
    clear like a loon.
I have kept within the music's beat
Swooped down low,
    yet staying right in tune.

I've sung that song
 and let my voice just soar
While deep within my soul
 the words brought tears
That slipped right down my cheeks;
    my heart just tore.

That song, reminding me
  of trials sore
Experienced by people
  who did so long
For freedom, justice, rights,
  and so much more.

The freedoms they had
  waited for too long.
I have been one acquainted
  with that song.

Modeled after "Acquainted with the Night"
by Robert Frost
April 2000

Ballad of William and Ann

Oh, it was around Christmas time
When the marriage,
   it was planned.
The family and friends
   all came to see
Lord William wed Lady Ann.

The musicians were seated,
   all playing their songs
Awaiting the groom to appear.
And seated among
   the guests that day
Sat his former love, Lady Mear.

The minister signaled
   the groom to come out
To stand with best man at the right.
The minister motioned
   the guests to stand
As the bride marched in
   dressed in white.

Lady Mear, she stood
   with hankie in hand
Weeping for the man she had lost.
She'd been too proud
   to accept the ring
Lord William had gotten at cost.

The bride advanced
   at a stately pace
By her handsome groom to stand.
Lady Mear, near an aisle,
   could be heard for a mile,
Shouting, "Hey, Lady Ann,
   that's my man!"

Lord William's response
   to the lady's outburst,
"You had my heart in your hand.
You cast me aside.
   Yes, I did love you first,
But today, I'll wed Lady Ann."

So that day long ago
   about Christmas time,
The guests got more
   than was planned.
An old love turned mean
   in quite a wild scene
When Lord William wed Lady Ann.

**Patterned after "Barbara Allen" Anonymous Poet

Waiting, Waiting, Waiting

Should we be happy or sad?
Should we be sorry or glad?

No more treatment.
No more meds.
Those doctors all have lost their creds.
No more stuff.
She's had enough.

*"Let me go!
You all must know
I've had a good life.
I've been a good wife
And a loyal mother.*

*"I've been a good sister
 to each dear brother.
A little demanding, yes that is true,
But, I've always been there
 for each of you.*

"Unhook the tubes.
      Detach each wire.
Bath me now and put me
    in a fresh gown.
Comb my hair and
    lay me back down.
        It's time *for me to retire.*

"I'm going home
    No more to roam
From doctor to doctor
    Looking for a cure.

      "I'm going Home
    Where a cure is sure."

      Should we be happy or sad?
      Should we be sorry or glad?

Phillis Wheatley Told Me

When they challenge your intellect,
Girl, fight back!

When they said, "You didn't write that?"
I said, "Really! What does it lack?"

They shouted right back.
"It's because you're black.
Blacks can't write like that!"

"Oh yeah!" I said.
(Maybe not just like that.)
"Watch my smoke
You better stay woke
'Cause I'm not through
With you -- or with you!"

I kept on writing, as I hope you do, too.

They'll believe when they see
Your intellect shine through,
That melanin is only a color of skin,
Not indicative at all of what you can do.

So, just keep on writing.
And when you're through,
They'll have to acknowledge
What you truly *did* do!

April, 2019

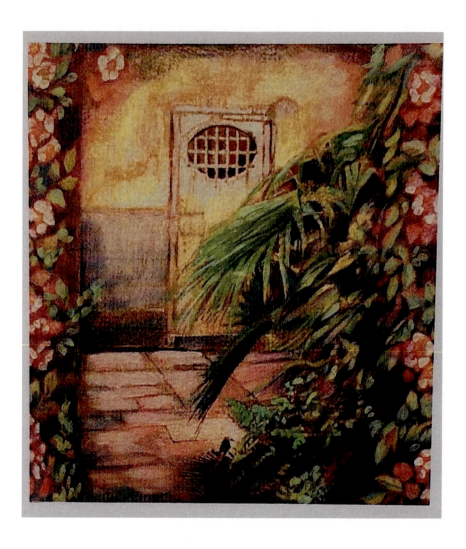

Garden Door
Deanna Denby Beye
Acrylic Mixed Media
10" x 12"

Garden Wall
Deanna Denby Beye
Acrylic Mixed Media
12" x 12"

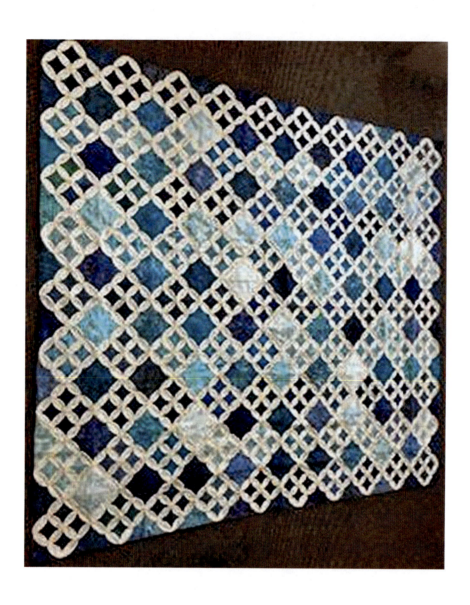

Cathedral Windows
Mary Clendeninn
Cotton Fabric
72" x 80"

January Gemstone: Garnet
Mary Clendeninn (MJ Kinman Design)
Mini-Quilt in Cotton Fabric
17" x 17"

Summer and Rootbeer
Moya Devine
Mixed Media on Museum Board
12" x 12"

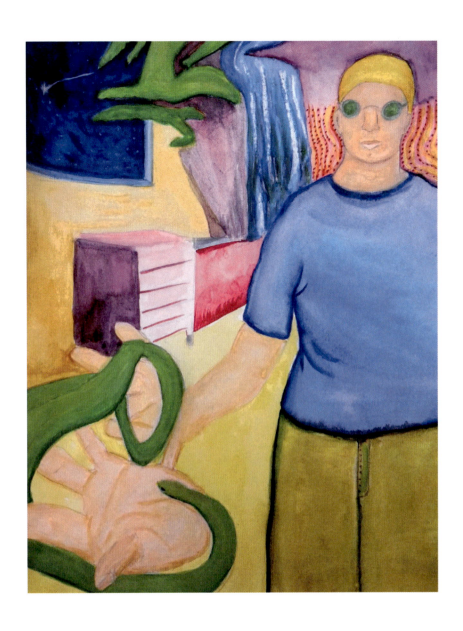

The Snake Charmer
Moya Devine
Mixed Media on Paper
11" X 14"

Native
Nicole Ellsworth
Colored Graphite Pencil on Paper
16" x 20"

Cascade
Nicole Ellsworth
Colored Pencil on Paper
16" x 20"

Falling Leaves
Annie Fang
Oil on Canvas
16" x 20"

Regression 2
Annie Fang
Acrylic on Canvas
16" x 20"

View from Clear Lake
Rachel Galarneau
Oil on Canvas
11" x 14"

Purple Haze
Rachel Galarneau
Oil on Canvas
11" x 14"

Summer Storm

Lightning flashing, slashing,
  bashing against sleeping eyelids.
Klieg lights turned on
  to spotlight the action.
Thunder crashing, thrashing,
  bashing against slumbering eardrums

Arousing those ignoring the call
  to watch whatever is at work.

Wind howling, scowling,
  prowling against the window,
Demanding attention
  to awesome power unleashed.

Midnight bright as the sun at noon-day.
Midnight loud as kids at play.

Adolescent trees bow in obeisance.
Ancient trees resist in vain.
Limbs thrown across the way
  like sticks
  in the hands of a giant
  playing catch and fetch with his dog.

Tempestuous teenager
  ripping off rooftops
Swiping them off
  with the flick of his wrist;
Tramping through the night at large,
Stomping up a storm,

  Then retreating off stage
  until enraged again.

      Or, is it God reminding us
          Who's really in charge?

Poor Pluto, Indeed!

That cry baby, Pluto!
What a nerve!
To think he could be one of us.
"Skedaddle, Pluto! Get lost!
Hit the road now, kid. Take a bus."

We're the Big Guys in the universe.
We're the ones in paintings and verse.
That little guy couldn't do the job.
Now he's got the nerve
  to sit there and sob.
Thought he could join us,
  but he's just a slob.

Look at Pluto at the edge of the galaxy,
Watching us whirl and what does he see?
Summer and winter, from June to June
Mars and Jupiter, Mercury and Neptune
Saturn, Uranus and Earth and Venus.
Yes, Pluto just wants to be whirling with us.

Poor, poor Pluto indeed!
We're the majestic Sequoias!
He's just a dwarf, a little skank weed.

"Get outta here, kid.
We're glad to be rid
Of a chump like you
Who didn't succeed.

Maybe in the future, you can join us then.
When you grow up and learn not to sob.
Now, get on the ball and go do your job.
We'll let you know. We'll tell you when."

Come on Big Guys.
We're the Celestial Gang,
Circling the sun and doing our thang.

Poor, poor Pluto, indeed!

Sounds on an Evening Walk

Click-clack of push mowers
Low buzzing of electric ones
Clip-snip of hand-held trimmers
Swish of broom
     sweeping the clippings

Purr of European sports cars
Rattle-ti-bang of teenager's clunker
Revving of motorcycle engines
Whirring of bicycle wheels on asphalt
Clackety-clatter of skateboards
     crossing the cracks in the sidewalk

Yip-yapping
of small dogs
Husky snarly, breathy growling
  of big ones
Heavy snorting
  through holes in fences
Padding back and forth
  on hard paw-packed yards
Chains dragging along to a snap

Gasp of dogs trying to get us,
Ha! But we're out of reach.

Summer 1987

Romeo Rap: Timeless and Timely

Cruising knightly with our homies
Hanging out much too late
Getting into so much trouble
Just because of hate

Reverend Joe, he's a minister,
Walking around our 'hood,
Warning us not to act so sinister
Saying we should be good.

"Get your learning,"
He would tell us.
"Each of you could be earning
More than you think you could,
More than you thought you would.
Now let's get going like you should.

"Don't be hanging with your crew
Doing what you should not do;
Staying out much too late
Attracting trouble because of hate.

"Come on, knights," he keeps on coaxing.
"Come on, knights," he keeps cajoling.
"Time to neutralize that hate.
Spread some good! It's not too late.

"Come on, knights," he keeps cajoling.
"Come on, knights," he keeps on coaxing.
"Time to neutralize that hate!
"Spread some good! It's not too late.

"It's time to neutralize that hate.
Let's spread some good! It's not too late!"

The Heart Tree

There's a tree in my heart
    Was it there at the start
Of my life as a wife and a mother,
Through the cares and woes
    And the joy that just goes
Along when one lives with another?

The trunk is my past,
    The part that will last
When the children have come and gone.
They are the branches --
    Reaching out, taking chances
Outside in the world and the throng.

This tree in my heart
I hope is a part
Of all I have known and still love.
It's trite, but it's true,
   But, the growth's due to you
Who grounded me in God's love above.

5 August 1995

Fist Fighting

She had quite a temper, that Anna.
Classmates and teachers couldn't stand'a.
When she got angry, she'd swing and hit ya.
Big or small, short or tall,
She'd just swing around and hit ya.

"Do not fight. It is not right.
Just turn the other check!"
"But Grammama, they'll tease me.
I don't want to look so meek."

"It's not right to fight. You can run away.
Meekness is strength under control," she'd say.
"Run away from a fight. I'll look like a fool!
Flight from a fight is not cool at school!"

"Control yourself. It's much more pleasing,
Even if they keep on teasing."

"But Grammama I have got to fight.
Every day they tease and taunt me
Saying I'm black, but I talk so white!"

So I fought and was caught
    and expelled from school
The day before graduation.
Depressed, in total desperation,
    saw I'd not been cool.
Fighting that guy created a big mess.
I cried, in the mirror in my first new dress.

I'd failed to stand up and failed to be strong.
Grammama was right all along.
It was not right to fight with fists.
I fought with my fists and look what I missed.

Turn the other cheek; it's okay to be meek.
Meekness is strength under control.
You'll have more peace within your soul.

You'll stand out in the throng as strong.
Yes, Grammama was right all along.

Fresh Off the Press
Nilly Gill
Oil on Canvas
10" x 8"

Heat
Nilly Gill
Tombow Pens on Acid Free Paper
8.5" x 5.5"

Belvedere
Therese Cipiti Herron
Oil and Carbon
36" x 48"

Summer
Therese Cipiti Herron
Acrylic and Carbon
36" x 48"

Letting Go
Ellie Hodges
Acrylic on Canvas
16" x 20"

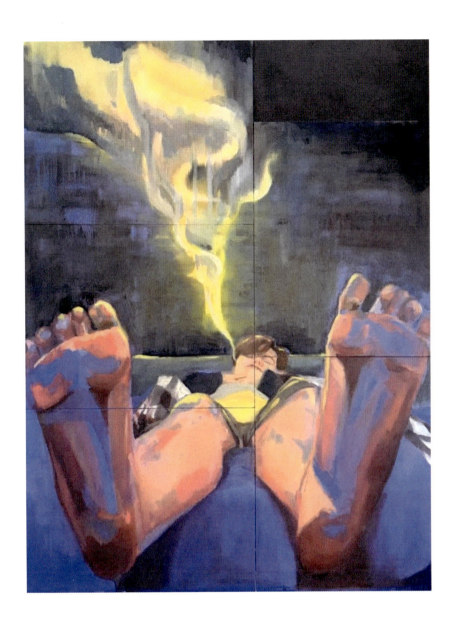

Self Portrait
Ellie Hodges
Oil on Canvas
22" x 28"

Rebel Youth
Nathan Huynh
Pen and Watercolor on Paper
16" x 20"

Distinguished Gentleman
Nathan Huynh
Pen and Watercolor on Paper
16" x 20"

Time Relative
Steven Kelly
Oil on Canvas
48" x 48"

Strands of Life
Steven Kelly
Oil on Canvas
48" x 48"

Submersion
Layla Khazeni
Acrylic on Canvas
9" x 12"

Recovery
Layla Khazeni
Acrylic on Canvas
9" x 12"

Torn
Luna Kostic
Acrylic on Paper
11" x 14"

Filter
Luna Kostic
Acrylic on Plexiglass with Digital Photography
5" x 7"

Memories
Laura Lehman
Mixed Media
18" x 25"

Drama
Laura Lehman
Mixed Media
12" x 12"

Grammama

Grammama was a powerful woman
Devoted to family and to God,
Best known for what she taught:
Walking the walk,
  not just talking the talk.

Devoted to family and to God,
Grammama got us to church weekly,
Walking the walk,
  not just talking the talk,
Grammama taught us
  to love by the Bible.

Grammama got us to church weekly
  To sing those hymns
  and hear the Word.
Grammama taught us
  to love by the Bible.
She loved it so much,
  she disciplined by it.

Grammama taught us
  to love by the a Bible.
  Best known for what she taught:
Walking the walk,
  not just talking the talk.
Grammama was a powerful woman.

*Jammie Elna Graham Williams (1899-1994)

Our Son

Robert, Bobby, Bob
  Fast, fleet, flown
    Baby, boy, grown

Born in a moment
  Walking at nine months
    Diving at two years
      Gymnast at twelve

On the move
  On the run
    Seldom sitting
      Often flitting
        Non-stop -- ready to drop

Flying on his Big Wheels
  Skidding under the bumper
    of our neighbor's Caddy
      Cheating death, but
        Barreling towards it

Building, building, building
   Wooden kindergarten blocks
      Golden Encyclopedia books
      Choreographing routines for
      cheerleading' bodies
Blocks, Books, Bodies

Seeing the patterns
   Finding the puzzle pieces, but
     Missing the picture

     Moving on
      Moving out
       Moving up

         High School
          Cheer Camps
           College

Kinko's in Sunnyvale
   Great Lakes Training in Illinois
      The Constellation in the Persian Gulf
      The Juneau in Sasebo, Japan

Cheerleader
   Choreographer
      Cook, Admiral's Chef
      Christian

On the move
   Flipping in time
      Hitting the groove
         Running out of time

Calling home
    "Dad" or "Daddy"
    "Mom" or "Mommy"
The mood determines the name.

"Help" or "Hooray!"
    Sunny or gray
        Seldom in between.

"Do I have to come home?"
    "Can I come home?"
        "I can't come home."
            "Now I have gone Home."

            Baby, Boy, Grown
            Robert, Bobby, Bob
            Fast, Fleet, Flown

25 August 2006

Visits

Military men had come,
with news no parent expects to hear.
"Ma'am, yesterday,
Navy officers in Sasebo, Japan
found your son in his apartment...
   dead.

He didn't show up to the ship.
They went to his apartment.
   They found him dead."

"My son is dead?
      He's never coming home!"

My son is dead!

In the twilight, I reel in limbo
In that haunting ground
Between dread of awake
    and terror of nightmare.

Tension tightens my neck
Flows down my back
Becoming a fiery fist
    at the base of my spine.

Fingers clutch the fragrant bed sheet;
Thighs stiffen into planks
And toes tingle like ice cubes.

That night...I lay in bed
   praying to process the news.

(An image appears...)

A doorway opens...
I recognize the place.
Bright light streams around two figures.
I recognize the people.

Standing there is my Grampoppa,
Light streaming all around
Haloed by light
Extending his hand in welcome.
"Come on in, son!" he says.

Behind him, my Grammama stands,
Peaking over his shoulder.
Her welcome smiles from her eyes.

"Come on in, son!" he beckons.

The voice is familiar.
   I'd heard it over the years.
Grampoppa said that when the uncles
   come home for Mother's Day Dinner.
 "Come on in, son!"
He said it at Father's Day
   and birthday gatherings.

"Come on in, son!"

Grampoppa and Grammama are there
  to greet my son!
To welcome him
  home with them
In heaven.
I believe it.

Heaven is home.
So, I'm content.

　　　I sigh and breathe.
　　　　　I believe it.
　　　　　　　All is well.

Bob is with Grampoppa
Bob is with Grammama,
All is well.

I sense another voice,

"Anna, my child. Your son is home.
And, see, he's Home with family."

    Ah, at last. Now at peace.
    Ah, at last. Not a peep.
      I drift into healing,
          comforting sleep.

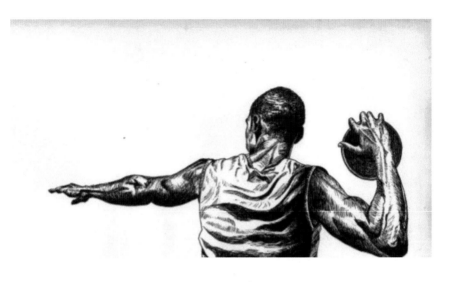

Track and Field
Christie Linnard
Ink on Paper
16" x 20"

Puffer
Christie Linnard
Ballpoint Pen on Canvas
9" x 12"

Communication
Linda Moe
Acrylic
22" x 24"

Old Road
Linda Moe
Watercolor
26.5" x 20"

The Wish
Thia Nevius
Monotype
22" x 31"

Three Friends
Thia Nevius
Watercolor
9" x 12"

Cut Up
Susan J. Osborn
Oil Pastel on Digital Photo Transfer
38" x 33"

Picador
Susan J. Osborn
Oil on Canvas
26" x 34"

Broken Pieces
Eric Pan
Oil on Canvas
16" x 20"

Grandfather Lǎo Yé
Eric Pan
Oil on Canvas
16" x 20"

Croc
Carlyssa Phoon
Watercolor and Gel Pen
16" x 20"

Bear
Carlyssa Phoon
Watercolor and Gel Pen
16" x 20"

Conduit #1
Stephen Steele
Acrylic, Mixed Media on Canvas
30" x 36"

Second Hand Rapture
Stephen Steele
Acrylic, Mixed Media on Canvas
48" x 48"

The Man Holes in His Socks

Sitting across from him on the sun porch
   Noticing those holes
   in the bottom of his socks,
Listening to the birds
   Chirping their evening reports
   to their parents,

Hearing the squawk of the ducks
   Teaching their ducklings
   to swim upstream,

I wonder what it would be like.

What would it be like
   to have no one to talk to,
   no one to report to,
   no one to tease about
the holes in the bottom of his socks;

   no one to interrupt my reading with,
"Hon. You've gotta listen to this." or
"Just a minute.
Have you heard this one?"

Listening to the roiling of the steam
   just outside the sunroom window,
Hearing the water tumble
   down the man-made rock croppings,
Pausing as the mourning doves coo
   across the way,

I wonder what it would be like.

What would it be like to be able
   to finish a chapter
   without being interrupted,
   without learning something new
   about something
   I never knew was important,
something I'd never
   even thought about before,

   without realizing
      how fortunate I am
      to hear from the man
      with the holes
      in the bottom of his socks, say

   "Babe. This won't take long?" or
   "Betcha never you hear this anymore."

Sitting across from him,
 I watch the sunbeams
     Streaming through the blinds,
     Slipping over his shoulder and
     Warming my toes,
     Signaling that day is ending,

I wonder what it would be like.

Then, I smile to myself,
     not having to wonder,
     glad I don't have to wonder,
     thrilled I don't have to wonder

What life would be like
 without the man with
 the holes in the bottom of his socks.

Summer, 2011
Published *in FINE LINES: August, 2016, Volume 25, Issue 3*, p. 214-15

Anniversary Poem

We have been married for over fifty years.
True, some of the days
   have been cool and blue,
But more have been bright, blazing gold.

Lying cradled in your arms,
I feel secure, cherished, and protected.
Engulfed in Grammama's
   handmade patchwork quilt.
Patches could symbolize the
   the five states in which we've lived,
     the three children we have borne,
      the myriad trips we've taken
        from the Atlantic to the Pacific
         in the car, or on a plane,
          on that Amtrak train.

What adventures we've shared!

You know I tease you
  about your holey socks,
    but it's wholly for fun.
I wish the same contentment
   in marriage for our children.

Sometimes when I see the deer scamper
   across the backyard,
I wonder if they enjoy their families
   as much as we do ours.

So, my dear, what lies ahead?

Whether smoky gray days
   or spicy peach days,
All will be better with you.

Living with the Bible keeps us in line.
I'm committed to you.
We'll be just fine.

Loyal friend, husband for life,
It's been my joy to be your wife.

The Evening Walk

Our walk begins on a smooth, flat sidewalk.
At the street corners is the gentle step-up,
    step down.
We discuss the day's events
    at a leisurely pace.

We turn the corner and begin
    the gentle incline;
No problem here.
    The heart beat is regular
A slight glow shines
    on our cheeks and foreheads.
Feet move along at a brisk pace.

Incline steepens - approaching the first hill
No problem.
    Heart beat speeds up.
    Perspiration beads gather.
Conversation slows down a bit.
Legs warm to the rhythm of the walk.

Final ascent of major hill
Problem.
    Heart beat visible through tee-shirt
    Sweat streams.
    Conversation gasps.
    Calves groan. Thighs burn.

Street sign, "500 feet to dead end"
    seems prophetic.

The sidewalk levels now and heart beat
    slows   down   a   bit
We pause a moment
    to wipe the moisture from faces.
We turn
        And
            Are speechless at the sight.

We are amazed
  by the panoramic view of San Diego
     From Miramar to Coronado!
The view unfolds in layers of colors
     First the red tile roofs of houses
     Grey-green tops of eucalyptus trees
     Brown green spread of the
        Naval air station
     Warm glowy-yellow of city lights
       sprinkled above
     Then the blue-black expanse of the night sky.

Moving east-to-west, airplanes
    approach Lindbergh Field.
Their twinkling red lights
    converge from separate legs
To the apex of a capital "A" lying on its side.

Arrayed above this,
    on the uppermost layer are
The constellations in all their splendor.
Everything is illuminated
    by the glimmer-shimmer of the moon.

    Rejuvenated,
We return home walking slowly down the hill,
    Revitalized
By the physical exertion of the steep climb,
    Relaxed
After the elation of the view from the top.

Self Portrait - Illiteracy
Sabrina Tian
Mixed Media
16" x 20"

Untitled
Sabrina Tian
Mixed Media
16" x 20"

La Clef (The Key)
Minnie Valero
Watercolor and Metal Key
15" x 10"

La Tranquera (The Gate)
Minnie Valero
Watercolor
11" x 14"

Cottage
Elizabeth Wepsic
Oil on Canvas
9" x 12"

Hidden Passage
Elizabeth Wepsic
Oil on Canvas
11" x 14"

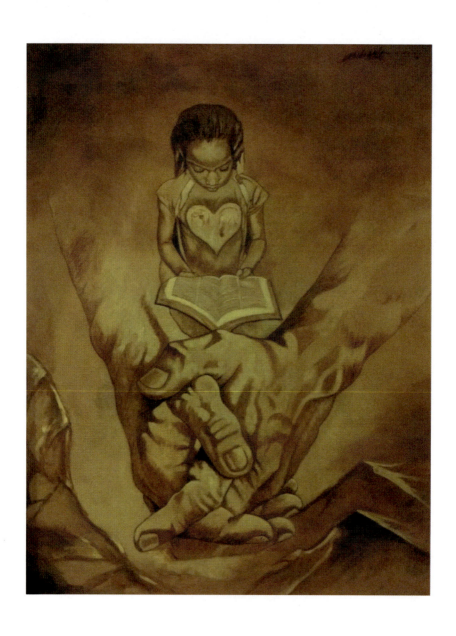

Shadow of Knowledge I
Lester White
Acrylic
47" x 36"

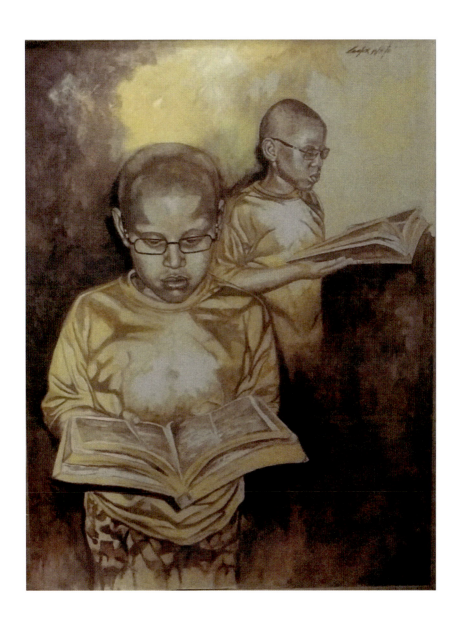

Shadow of Knowledge II
Lester White
Acrylic
41" x 32"

Walking to the Game
Nancy White
Photo Manipulation
8" x 10"

Ireland
Nancy White
Photo Manipulation
8" x 8"

Map #1
Marcus Woolley
Colored Pencil on Paper
9" x 12"

Map #2
Marcus Woolley
Colored Pencil on Paper
9" x 12"

Depreciated
Sharisa You
Acrylic on Canvas
16" x 20"

Floral Dance
Sharisa You
Pastel
16 x 20"

Yes, You Are!

You are good!
It's okay to be good all alone.
So, just keep on doing what you should
To bring joy to yourself
And share joy with others.

You are kind!
It doesn't matter
If we don't understand
When you do what you should
To bring peace to yourself
And share peace with others.

You are smart!
We just may be jealous
When you get accolades.

So, keep doing what you should
To bring to light to yourself
And to share your light with others.

April, 2019

*Painting is silent poetry, and
poetry is painting that speaks."*
Plutarch

REFLECTING on Experiences with Poems and Pictures

Entering Art to Write
Exploring Poems to Create Art

Let the pictures speak to you.

Write what you experience
 when you view the artwork.

Try some of the writing
 activities that follow.

Let the poem tell you what to create.

Paint, sketch, draw, quilt, or plan
 photographs of what you experience
 when you read the poems
 silently and out loud.

Entering Art and Writing About It

Experience ways this imaginative entry evokes all five senses, memories, and dreams .

Notice what you see; look and allow yourself to feel and imagine.

Give yourself lots of time for the various exercises to have experiences that are personal and uniquely your own.

Take time to put experience into words and thus enrich both your own viewing and the work of art itself.

Try several of the options.
See which you enjoy more.

Step inside the artwork.

What does it feel like as you journey into the picture? Let its space become your space.
- Where are you?
- What do you hear?
- What do you smell?
- What do you notice under your feet?

Imagine you can touch something in the artwork.
- What would that be?
- How would it feel?

Write about the artwork as if it were a dream.
- Bring the scene to life and leave us in that moment.
- Use "In a dream, I ...." or "Last night I had the strangest dream ...." or, simply, "I dreamed...."

Write about the scene as if it is happening now, using present tense and active verbs.
- Begin with "I am …." Move around inside the work and make things happen.
- Begin a line with "Suddenly …." in order to create surprise, moving into something unexpected.

Write about the artwork as if it is a memory. List short, separate memories or one long memory. Both invent and remember as you write.

Imagine the art as something you see outside a window. Begin with "From my window, I see …."

Adapted from "Entering Art", a workshop led by Terry and Jenny Williams at the Detroit Institute of Art.

Experience Poems and Pictures

Writing Stories about Pictures

Have some fun and expand your notes into a poem, narrative fiction or essay for which your chosen picture can be an illustration.

Answer these questions as you consider your poem, story, or narrative essay:

Who will be your main character?

- **Human** – adult, teen, child, infant
- **Animal**, bird, fish, insect, other
- **Alien**

When will your narrative take place?

- **Time of day**: dawn, morning, afternoon, evening, night
- **Time of year**: winter, spring, summer, fall
- **Time in life**: childhood, teen years, adult, senior years of your main character
- **Time in history**: pre-historic, medieval, Elizabethan Age, future

Where will your story take place?

- **Area of place**: inside, outside, porch, roof, basement , cellar, other
- **Locale**: city, country, mountains, sea, valley, forest
- **Continent**: Africa, Asia, Europe, North or South America, Antarctica, or Australia
- **Galaxy**: Earth, another planet, another galaxy

What is the problem to be solved in your narrative?

- Physical, intellectual, magical, spiritual, other.
- Inside the character?
- Between character and someone or something else.
- Combination

Who or what is the main character struggling against?

- another **character**
- a force of **nature** — weather, thirst, illness, or topography (desert, mountain, roiling rapids)
- a **group** of people acting as one — a team, racial group, pack of peers, political party, social club, or ethnic tribe
- a **ghost**, an **alien**, the **gods**, or a **Supreme Being** as may be seen in myths, religious or fantasy fiction
- struggle with a **machine**, like a car, tractor, tank, android, or computer that may occur in real life or science fiction

How will main character solve the problem?
- **Physically?**
- **Mentally?**
- **Magically?**
- **Spiritually?**
- **Combination?**

Writing a Pantoum Poem*
about a Picture

Begin by writing four original lines about the artwork.
(1)_____
(2)_____
(3)_____
(4)_____

Repeat lines 2 and 4, and add lines 5 and 6 to expand ideas introduced in lines 2 and 4.
(2)_____
(5)_____
(4)_____
(6)_____

Repeat lines 5 and 6, and add lines 7 and 8 to expand ideas mentioned in lines five and six.

(5)_____
(7)_____
(6)_____
(8)_____

Finally, repeat lines 1, 3, 7 and 8 in this order:

(7)_____
(3)_____
(8)_____
(1)_____

What words, phrases, or punctuation need to be changed to make your poem flow?

* See "Gramamma" on page 64

Experience Poems and Pictures

Exploring Poems to Create Art

Try this with colors in a **medium** of your choice: oil, water colors, gouache, acrylics, clay, pen and ink, pieces of paper or cloth, or camera.

Go back and reread the poems. Choose those that speak to or resonate with you.

Consider these questions:

- What colors could represent the **mood**, or way you feel when you read the poem?
- What colors seem to represent the **tone**, or way the poet seems to feel about the topic in the poem?
- What colors has the poet mentioned? Do you think those represent the tone or mood of this poem?
- What **texture**(s) will you use?
- What **shapes**(s) will you use?

- If the poem were a **speech in a play**, who would be saying these lines? What colors would the character be wearing?

- If the poem described a **setting in a movie**, what colors would you choose to be used in the set?

- If you were the **illustrator** of this book, what picture(s) in this book would you include on the pages to reflect or represent the words of the poem(s) you've chosen?

Now experiment, choosing the artistic style of your choice: realistic (representational), cubist, impressionistic, or abstract. Or pattern the work of an artist in a school of painting that appeals to you such as baroque, chiaroscuro, idealism or realism, impressionism, pop art, art deco, abstract, art nouveau, post-impressionism, etc.

And, please share your artwork with those you love.

Contributors' Websites

See more of their work.
Visit our artists' websites.

Artist	Website
Jayamini Attanayake	www.fiverr.com/jayamini25
Moya Devine	www.moyadevine.com
Therese Cipiti Herron	www.TereseFineArt.com
Steven Kelly (Smith)	www.stevenkgallery.com
Laura Lehman	www.lauralehman.com
Thia Nevius	www.ThiaArtist.com
Susan J. Osborn	www.osbornart.com
Carlyssa Phoon	Instagram.com/Carlyssa.Ph/
Minnie Valero	www.minnievalero.com
Elizabeth Wepsic	www.elizabethwepsic.com

Poet: Anna J. Small Roseboro
www.gettingstartedgettinggoing.org
www.teachingenlishlanguagearts.com

Made in the USA
Middletown, DE
24 June 2019